Testament in Black

Testament in Black

BY

Brandon Iwan

Copyright © 2023, Brandon Iwan

All rights reserved. Printed in the U.S.A.

No part of this publication may be reproduced or transmitted in any form or by any means, electronic or mechanical, including photocopy, recording or any information storage and retrieval system now known or to be invented, without permission in writing from the publisher, except by a reviewer who wishes to quote brief passages in connection with a review written for inclusion in a magazine, newspaper or broadcast.

Quantity Purchases:
Companies, professional groups, clubs, and other organizations may qualify for special terms when ordering quantities of this title. For information, email info@ebooks2go.net, or call (847) 598-1150 ext. 4141.
www.ebooks2go.net

Published in the United States by eBooks2go, Inc.
1827 Walden Office Square, Suite 260,
Schaumburg, IL 60173

ISBN: 978-1-5457-5714-7

Library of Congress Cataloging in Publication

Table of Contents

Verse 1	Gate of Frost	1
Verse 2	Cathedral of Thorns	2
Verse 3	Hungry Earth	3
Verse 4	Soul of Iron	4
Verse 5	Stench of Decay	5
Verse 6	Rite of Fire	6
Verse 7	Weeping Star	7
Verse 8	Revenant	8
Verse 9	Altar of Blood	9
Verse 10	Crown of Bones	10
Verse 11	Sweet Suffering	11
Verse 12	City of Worms	12
Verse 13	Not Worth Saving	13
Verse 14	Rising Hope	14
Verse 15	Blood of Fear	15
Verse 16	Furious Hate	16
Verse 17	Mind of Madness	17
Verse 18	Fallen Leaf	18
Verse 19	Scorched Soul	19
Verse 20	Evil Mind	20
Verse 21	Angry Sky	21
Verse 22	Shadow of Rust	22

Verse 23	Undeath I Am	23
Verse 24	Veil of Darkness	24
Verse 25	Piercing Eyes	25
Verse 26	Twilight of Despair	26
Verse 27	Pale Light	27
Verse 28	Fallen Night	28
Verse 29	Sins of the Father	29
Verse 30	Stairway to Damnation	30
Verse 31	Dead Time	31
Verse 32	In the Dark of Doom	32
Verse 33	Unholy Living	33
Verse 34	Grave Alive	34
Verse 35	Wrath and Malice	35
Verse 36	Riddle of Rage	36
Verse 37	Midnight Sun	37
Verse 38	Angel's Ash	38
Verse 39	Empty Soul	39
Verse 40	Offering	40
Verse 41	Lord of Death	41
Verse 42	Curse of the Fallen	42
Verse 43	Shadows of the World	43
Verse 44	Sickness	44
Verse 45	Failing Light	45

Verse 46	Sleepless Dream	46
Verse 47	Coven of the Wicked	47
Verse 48	Mysterium	48
Verse 49	Ever Be Dead	49
Verse 50	Locked Gate	50
Verse 51	Hour of Judgment	51
Verse 52	Question of Life	52
Verse 53	Unholy Blessing	53
Verse 54	Beyond Understanding	54
Verse 55	Shadow of Despair	55
Verse 56	Beyond Reality	56
Verse 57	Might of Madness	57
Verse 58	Black Vile	58
Verse 59	Leach on Life	59
Verse 60	Frozen Fire	60
Verse 61	Spirit of the Abyss	61
Verse 62	Beneath Light	62
Verse 63	Bleeding Soul	63
Verse 64	Fallen World	64
Verse 65	Life and Decay	65
Verse 66	River of Black	66
Verse 67	Tainted Land	67
Verse 68	Dark Shade	68

Verse 69	Despicable Rise	69
Verse 70	Bone of Evil	70
Verse 71	Fury of Anger	71
Verse 72	Dark of Damnation	72
Verse 73	Flesh Puppets	73
Verse 74	Malevolence	74
Verse 75	Frozen Fire Burning Ice	75
Verse 76	Forbidden Scriptures	76
Verse 77	Unseen Light	77
Verse 78	Sinking Star	78
Verse 79	Voice of the Cursed	79
Verse 80	Damnation Rise	80
Verse 81	Break Their Soul	81
Verse 82	In the Name of Death	82
Verse 83	Vile	83
Verse 84	Blood and Bone	84
Verse 85	Lost Rhymes	85
Verse 86	Final Testament	87

Verse 1

Gate of Frost

Across the road with frozen dust beneath your feet, arise ethereal mist. This will guide you down the road to the path unknown. Follow the glow of the mist; it will lead you to the end. Heed the warning to not veer from the guidance of the mist. Listen not to the calls of chattering spirits, for they will lead you to the lost. Keep pushing forth with what courage you have; keep it close. Gather your footing for you approach the river of ice. Gaze forth and tread lightly. Do not disturb the water. Now you have reached the other side. You are getting close, for the end is coming. Follow the mist through the barrows. Proceed with great caution lest you be lost with the spirits beneath the frozen earth. Let the mist take you to the end, for you have reached the gate of frost. Follow the mist through the gate and claim your prize, for it is the end.

Verse 2

Cathedral of Thorns

Through the darkness of the moors lies a church. With many spires crowning the sacristy and the nave, like an iron crown of king full malice.
The gates open to welcome those who have made the journey. Inside, the stench of incense and decay fill the air. The pews of rotted wood lay bare, but if only the books of old written in a tongue unknown spread across the pews. Upon the ground, scattered shards of broken glass were strewn about the floor, with no windows to be seen. Within these walls a hollow chant is heard, "Sacred is nothing; nothing is sacred." Upon the altar a book lies open as the priest steps forward, clothed in robes of purple and gold. He addresses the congregation with no parishioners to be seen, for the service is dead, and to be in his service is to be dead.

Verse 3

Hungry Earth

Walk down the forest road, down the path of everlasting. Through the branches of dead trees, a clearing comes in sight. Approach the field of crimson soil where innocent blood was spilled. Through the silence, the howls of the forsaken bellow up. The ground begins to quake as fissures open. Arms reach out through the mud as the hollows echo louder, screaming for one to listen, all in vain. The stars and moon are veiled as silence returns. All became calm if not for a deathly laughter, for they have returned to the realm beneath the earth.

Verse 4

Soul of Iron

The gears that grind the wheels of life into motion have now rusted to a halt. Darkness comes as the flames of hope flicker into shadow. In this being, the mind decays to a sickly form. Ears go deaf; eyes go blind. For what has been seen and what has been heard have sent the brave mind into madness, the souls that remain rust and turn to dust. The chilling wind blows the soulless dust to a plain unvented. And let it be that the cycle starts again, last as it was first.

Verse 5

Stench of Decay

Come forth and behold, a hollow grave peering down to a void not seen. Gaze upon the ground of putrefaction, gaze and see the corpses rot in the land of decomposition. The earth trembles with worms of great hunger. Come and feed your famished bodies, for the dead no longer need their own. Let the crows feast upon the hanging flesh, for their bones have abandoned it. Take a breath and breathe in the stench of decay.

Verse 6

Rite of Fire

Night has fallen as the light dims; it is time for the cleansing to begin. A man wanders clothed in robes of black, red, and gold. Down the hall to the chamber he enters the room awaiting the presence of this seeker. In the center of the room with a pale flame at his feet, the man sheds all clothes until bare naked he stands. Looming up he speaks, "Abandon your body," and the flame arose. "Abandon your mind" the fire still grows, "abandon your soul" the flames rage. Dawn breaks as embers fall, then to smoke. The sun rises to a silent day.

Verse 7

Weeping Star

The lonely man stares up at the sky with frost in his eyes, with a fleeting hope that someone is looking back to wipe his frozen tears away. Veiled are the stars and the moon. Clouds of black and gray push the sun away. Yet still, the man looks upward with a flicker of hope. Soon to realize there is no light to be seen. But at this hour the clouds part to reveal a hopeless void and a sun frozen, crying out looking down; the tears of stars cover the world in frozen fire.

Verse 8

Revenant

The bells ring a hollow chime, for the hour grows late. At this the hour of darkness's great design, a shadow rises from the mist; a shade of malice and despair takes shape. The form taken from the spirits of empty souls; it lurches forward. With shadow and darkness, it creeps across the land as the earth withers beneath its presence. Its breath is of decay, and madness be its gaze. Focus all eyes into emptiness to see the truth of what it has to offer, like a cold mist that rises up, and so it shall fall. As all light and life in this world, it rises only to fall.

Verse 9

Altar of Blood

Let the lost approach the church with great thirst. The doors open and so come in and bask in the sweet smell of crimson iron. Revel in red, the glow that reflects true desire. Join us at the altar, and have a taste of the blood of sacrifice, and feed your craving for this sinful drink, "Enjoy every drop." Let desire take you as the sacrifice is made. Watch on as the wicked souls are bled upon the great stone altar. Let the blood of their suffering satisfy the thirst of vile intent. Drink and join the damned.

Verse 10

Crown of Bones

A black shape rises from the marsh with a sickly glow. Atop of this forgotten shadow lay a crown of shattered bones, "A crown fitted for a king of the fallen." The king marches forward, if king he was, for all he has is lost. Over the marshes a tomb of broken stone is seen. The fallen king enters the tomb and sees the body of a mighty man clad in gold and jewels but no crown. The fallen king looks on at this man to realize what he once was, a mighty king, now reduced to shade and broken bones. For the broken shall forever be broken, and the mighty shall forever be mighty.

Verse 11

Sweet Suffering

Piercing flesh and broken bones, a sanction of ever-present and everlasting pain. Glide the blade across the vein, oh the greatest pleasure of pain. Twisted mind, twisted flesh. Suffering be my way, agony be my joy. Unstitch these eyes only to see a despicable world. This world will see as we have seen that the truth of sweet suffering is pleasure, for living is true suffering.

Verse 12

City of Worms

Abandon the body, flesh, and mind. There is no place for life in the city where all is lost. Voices fill the spires and bells chime to call the wary to be welcomed in and leave the world behind. Shed your human body, for the earth needs to feed. Ascend to the iron tower and follow the chatterers to the top. Gaze down at the earth as it comes alive with ravenous hunger. Come and consume the living; the earth belches, as it is now satisfied. Looking down and seeing what is left behind, for thou are blessed.

Verse 13

Not Worth Saving

Look up and see the blackness as shadows crawl over all life. Looking down, the world is falling to the path of nothingness. All that is sacred is burned to ash, innocence defiled as the priest is drunk on the sacrament. The mothers are killing their sons, and the fathers are killing their daughters. The world spins in a cyclone of madness and twisted forms of what was once holy. All is worthless; all is sickness. This world is not worth saving.

Verse 14

Rising Hope

Kindled hearts, worm inside. When all is lost still push on. But a warning left unheard tells to be wary of the unseen. Yet in this blissful peace a corruption begins to rise in their hearts, then to their souls. Their light slowly dims as corruption sets in, bringing dread, doubt, and despair. But in this dark, hope will rise. Warm turns to cold, embers to ash. Though hope rises to the land of abundance, casting aside those who have forsaken the blessed embers of hope. So now they wander meaningless and without purpose. Let punishment be poured out; hope rises, darkness falls, and let it be so.

Verse 15

Blood of Fear

There is an overcoming and everlasting horror that floods the veins of the brave. So cold, so alone, so dark, gripped by a terror one cannot escape. The mind is driven into madness by a dark terror beyond mortal comprehension. Release me! Release me! The tormented cry out with not an ear to hear or a mind to listen. Let the soul bleed and embrace salvation. Slumber as fear pours out. At last the nightmare out from the restless mind enters now the serenity of eternal sleep.

Verse 16

Furious Hate

Behold! The world shall be consumed by the flames of fury. Behold! The roads a river of blood spilled by the hand of anger might. None is safe, none is spared, for every man and woman, young and old, must be sacrificed into fire. Let their ashes rise as the sky bleeds red. Nothing survives as hatred rises. The frozen fire burning day and night, the cries of pain ring out, echoing a melody of a furious hate.

Verse 17

Mind of Madness

Released from reality, the enlightened ones forsake the lies of this world to let the voices of the mind guide them on the path. Twisting, turning the calls of chattering spirits cry out in a blissful tune of confusion. Let all fall around, for in the mind the world holds no meaning. Eyes open all around to see the world in madness, only so, for the madness in the world is the madness conceived in the mind enlightened, now far gone.

Verse 18

Fallen Leaf

The hour grows late, and the trees shake with frigid fright, as the sun sets on a cold night. Upward a pale light dims from a sinking moon clinging ever so desperately to the sky. The trees tremble in the cold wind of the night. The pale light of the moon reflects the withering of nature that surely draws near. Tree branches cling to hope that the dawn will come, and surely it shall. The sun rises to witness that all have died and the warmth that came, came too late. The last leaf falls from the tree, like a tear from a sad oak. The desolation of nature will banish the sun to an endless night.

Verse 19

Scorched Soul

Within the state of being an ember is kindled, destined to arise to a flickering flame. Within the conscience of the soul, warmth returns to an eager life. The eye can see again to gaze at the light once more. As peace returns, the flame inside grows higher and hotter like the coals of a blacksmith's forge. Higher and hotter the flames grow, a fire now out of control. A soul once with a comforting warmth, now burns with sinful pain. The flame thought to bring peace was a bringer of lies. Forever the soul will burn until the ravage of time has had its way.

Verse 20

Evil Mind

The time has come. Burning the pages of sacred thoughts, defiling purity as the darkness within is released. The blood of the holy is poured out, spilled by the vagrant wicked. Let evil manifest itself and take shape. Let the embodiment of the darkest of thoughts and desires be released from its chains clasped on by the holy ones. Unleash the darkness upon the world, for who can stop it? What can contain it? Because evil is in all of us, you need only to look inside the mind.

Verse 21

Angry Sky

Clouds gather in a spiral of swirling madness as thunder roars with a crackling fury. Lightning splits, the sky to scorch the earth with unholy wrath. Call down rocks of razor blades to rend flesh from bone. All shall be smiting down in rage and anger. The clouds crash to earth and tear apart the land. With the world in ruin, the sky looks down in great pleasure and satisfaction.

Verse 22

Shadow of Rust

The final whistle blows at the late hour of the day to usher in the night. The gears of the iron works grind to a halt as the laborers retire. The light of the molten iron fades into memory as all goes silent. Night has fallen with no one to manage the works of the factory. The whistle has blown the last and final time. The laborers are never to return, the foreman leaving all behind. The factory produces no longer. Now time has claimed the factory, and when rust grows deep in the gears, the assembly line will forever show the fate of a neglected and abandoned machine. As is a neglected and abandoned soul.

Verse 23

Undeath I Am

Hear my voice and obey! Rise from your eternal slumber, rise to me from the underneath. Gather your bones now unbroken. Gather your flesh made new by my hand. Hear the words of my voice, as it is time to take back what is yours; it is time to take back from the living who have forsaken you. Go forth and spread eternal rot, and reduce their cities to ruin, for in the wake of undeath none shall be spared. Their end has come. The living will die, and the dead will rise forever. This is the will from below.

Verse 24

Veil of Darkness

The sun shines so bright and pure. Pure is the light with radiance of hope to kindle life for all the people. This holy light banishes the darkness out of this world. The darkness stands alone, in a cold void. Because as darkness is gone, corruption lives on in the hearts of all who do not accept the light. The people of this world grow hungry for more, more than what the holy flame has given. Their greed and lust for more than what they deserve lead them to seek other forms of satisfaction. The people have given themselves to an unclean path. The light has been rejected as the holiness passes on into death and defeat. Embrace the darkness, for this is your reward.

Verse 25

Piercing Eyes

Within the dark, eyes of a thing unseen shine with an unsettling glow that can be seen by all if only their eyes can see it. The ones with no sight have eyes that glow with fury and malice. The ones whose eyes that cannot see light glow bright blue with weeping crystals, as they are forever lost. The eyes of the black abyss gaze into the eyes of the weak, to bring fear and dread. But only the sight of the great eye thrusts its gaze through all others. For the right eye of the one above meets the left eye of the one below.

Verse 26

Twilight of Despair

The sun sets on a quiet night, closing the shades of the main chamber of the house; a candle light is all that is seen. The master sits in his chair to reflect and rename. Closing his eyes, the master rocks back and forth. As he rocks forward looking to the past, he sees the anger, a hate that has befallen him, lost love and broken promises. He rocks back to view the future, only to see nothing but a black void. Back and forth he rocks for what seems like years. Nothing remains for him. The candle goes out and all to dust.

Verse 27

Pale Light

Walking down the corridors of winding halls the old man follows the light, glowing ever so dim. The light guides him through an iron door. As the door opens, a room of books old, new, forgotten, and restored, lay about. But for all the knowledge around him, the old man is fixed on the light of the lantern at the end of the room. Ignoring power, ignoring knowledge, and ignoring desire he picks up the lantern to see his life reflected in the glow. A single tear runs down his face. He is now at peace.

Verse 28

Fallen Night

Dusk approaches, and the castle gate opens. A man clad in armor of silver and gold and set upon a horse of great majesty sets forth. The great night pushes onward into the shadow, to the foe he must face. The night's armor shines in the dark, but emulates nothing. But at last he confronts his foe. A night clad in black iron, covered in blood, he lunges forth and the two engage in battle. At last, the night of silver and gold thrusts his sword through his enemy. Victorious he rides back to find the castle gate is locked. The mighty warrior looks up at the sky and sees night has fallen.

Verse 29

Sins of the Father

The midnight mass has ended, and the church grows quiet as the doors lock shut. The priest clears the altar to indulge in a sacrament of his own. The priest drinks the sacred wine and stuffs his face with the holy bread. With his belly full to burst and drunk on his gluttonous sin, he stumbles to the back of the church to snuff out the candles and leave all behind. Stumbling forward too drunk to see that his robes had caught fire from being too close to the flame he set to extinguish. The flames crawl across his body until nothing but a charred corpse remains. The priest to confession, confession to judgment, judgment to eternity.

Verse 30

Stairway to Damnation

Follow the desert path, and come close for the ones unknown are calling you to come forth. "Join us," they say, as you, the one owes our pleasure. "We wish to share this blissful journey"; follow the path across the road to nothing. Now before thee is the road leading to an endless stairway, "You have come," the voices say. Come and claim your prize! Fire rages up; cries ring out. Giving into lies, now fall down to destruction, into madness, and forever restlessly writhe in the damnation that has been chosen.

Verse 31

Dead Time

Time users in death and as such shall heal no wounds. The man who thinks time is on their side is a fool. Nothing is ageless, so be that time draws one closer to their final fate. And so in the timeless halls souls wander aimlessly. For the fate of man is to age and die, die and rebirth. We are to suffer this fate until the wheels of time are ground to dust and blown away; we will then be at peace.

Verse 32

In the Dark of Doom

Witness the sun fallen in the hand of darkness. Watch as the darkness brings chaos, war and pain, for none will see the light. War and devastation will set in motion, the machine of life's demise. The sun will never rise again. Only the weeping moon with tears of boiling blood rises high in the blackened sky and reveals death and carnage. True dark is all that remains, for the veil has fallen and all shall be lost, as the doors of doom lay wide open and the gates of the blessed are shut.

Verse 33

Unholy Living

We are wrenched, forsaken by light. We seek no sanctuary, no pity, no mercy. We claim our strength from our inner most rot, as our cycle of hate fuels our drive. Our flesh will be renewed by the blood of the pure. We will drink the agony of those who cast us aside. No place for them above, no place for them below. This world is ours. We shall live because they must die.

Verse 34

Grave Alive

From graves are born a mass of worms of a hunger not satisfied. From the masses of the earth arise a vengeful flesh. From a sinking star the brothers of the earth rise upward and onward, as the dance of death begins. At the hour of the witch, the feast can now begin. Feasting on rotted flesh torn from bone, for their bodies, of their brothers provide the nourishment until they can't eat no more. But there is one who has not partaken in the dance or the feast; the earth comes to life and the grave reclaims its prize. Now the worms of the grave can feast once more.

Verse 35

Wrath and Malice

All must die! All must fall! Let this world bleed. Let this world burn. Absolute be our wrath; everlasting be my malice. May this world be lost in fire and the living bleed and die by our hand. Their flesh will be shredded and their bones will be shattered, in my presence now know true suffering. Their life is gone, and their hope wasted. There is no peace, no love, no joy; suffering is all that remains. No more will any one look to hope, or any joyful voice sing. The world will burn in unholy fire as darkness falls on a bed of emptiness.

Verse 36

Riddle of Rage

We will feast upon your flesh, upon your blood, upon your soul, for all you are shall burn in the furnace of doom. None but eternal darkness and pain, see your miserable life is all in vain. Stomp upon the road of skulls. We will gouge and tear them all. Spilling their guts onto the floor. Consume their life with bleeding gore. Open the veins of their immortal souls and burn to ash and blackened coal. Let it be known your doom is not coming, it is already here.

Verse 37

Midnight Sun

The clouds gather, and the sky trembles. The twilight hour has come, for daylight has come to die. The stars fall and the moon is veiled with a crimson shade, for the moon's light reflects the blood that has been spilled. At this hour, we raise a glass high to the cries of the crimson moon. Released from the chains of purity that reveal the despair illuminated by the reflections of red. Let us dance, let us sing in what glory the red moon has brought onto us. Grateful are we, who have taken part in the drink of crimson night.

Verse 38

Angel's Ash

Let their wings be burned to ash, let their spirit be shattered, stain their robes with the blood of their brothers. Let them be dragged down, these wretched hypocrites, for they deserve no mercy of pity. These pampered and privileged ones will know what it is to be humbled through pain. They are so foolish to see their actions led to their ultimate end. It is to be known that the wolves will take their flesh, the flies cover their bones, and fire rises up to claim their spirit. The oppressed dance in the ashes, with glee and satisfaction are they set free.

Verse 39

Empty Soul

Step into the dark, and behold, the red moon rises. Come forth and witness as the light fades ever faster. Look and take warning and gaze upon the suffering of the damned. Look and see the boastful vermin, the ones that take and give nothing. Listen to the black and wretched sermon. Open the mind to witness the soulless heart; only dark remains. There is no hope because the soul is hollow. Take in all to feed the emptiness but all shall starve. Lifeless light is all that remains. In the dark there is nothing, so in the dark be reborn.

Verse 40

Offering

Become as the one to take part in this most blissful experience. The sacrifice will begin, and soon the chosen must bleed. The blood of sacrifice is lit on fire, filling the air with smoke of cleansing. Take in the smoke of that has been offered to us in ritual. The soul is filled with vapors of the one burned for us to indulge in a great desire to seek and to feed our lust for power. The power over man, the power of this greatest offering will let those who partake and gain everything. We shall return when the world is anew, and take it all with the sacrifice and offering of the chosen few.

Verse 41

Lord of Death

The lord of death arrives in the darkest night to stretch the shadow across the land. Black and cold are his hands; he comes from winds of the frozen north. With talons of steel he reaps the soul, he tears the heart, and turns the flesh to frosted ash. He brings wrath to the world in the form of withered fields, sickness, and plague. An endless winter of dark decay, where no light will be seen again. The shadow of his will shall last forever throughout eternity. Let all who live die by his hand.

Verse 42

Curse of the Fallen

Rise up, oh spirits of unearthly rage. Fill the living with their cursed unlife. The anger of the spirits from far beyond runs strong, for they had been done wrong. None had honored them in life, but in death they live on. They seek a vengeful justice, as this is their salvation. Extending their unseen world influence across the world, for all to fall only to rise to join them in misery. What the world has forsaken will now consume the living to be slaves as the fallen ones had once been. Raise your bones because victory is now yours.

Verse 43

Shadows of the World

This world is full of many dark places, which light cannot pierce. Within the darkness one just might find the truth to what they seek. Even if the truth can come at a terrible cost, they still seek out the darkness in a folly attempt to see the light. In the dark illuminated by the dead light in the eyes of the wicked, we can see the fate that will befall their foolish journey for forbidden wisdom. The wicked turn to shadow, losing their body, memory, and mind. Even for all their claims of power and knowledge they do not have the wisdom to see that the darkness never will reveal secrets to anyone. So come in; I have so much to show you.

Verse 44

Sickness

The screams of the sickly fill the sky, and the howls of the lonely hear them cry. Out of the ashes they rise with the sight of a thousand pale eyes. They will see the end of everything when the bells chime a dismal ring. Kings of old, kings of the fallen clutch their frosted crown.
I wonder who hears them cry? Can a mind conceive behind the weary and sad eyes? Strings of a fading hope in shade, come forth and find the path of the sickly road leading to the final outcome. Hear the call from below; hear the call and let it be so.

Verse 45

Failing Light

Should the light fade to frost, should the embers rise, should the embers fall, puppets pull the strings on the master's crumbling wings. A riddle to guess if one can see the end of everything. Hear the cries coming from eternity, coming forth only to die. When light dims to dismay, all shall fall and fade. Though in the dark a light still shines. The last light called hope. Darkness encroaches but cannot touch the light. Hope is kindled and shall remain until when all is forgotten and everything light and dark, life and death, good and evil is no more.

Verse 46

Sleepless Dream

Awake from the nightly slumber with shadows all around, twisting and turning, falling in and out of shape, to draw the attention to the call of the night. Shaking off the nightmare that befell the one who turned away the dawn, and welcomed in the setting sun, will see no light. Sun and stars will sink to shade when shadows rise again. Cold is the night and warm is the comfort of the bed. The eyes grow heavy and soon shut. Wakening again to the shadows and shade, stuck in a timeless age of a wakening slumber, find no rest in endless night.

Verse 47

Coven of the Wicked

Fix one's gaze and stare into eyes of the wicked; witness the witch's singing, chanting. Fix all eyes into the eye of the abyss, watch where holy light is banished and frozen breath chills the soul. The liars cling to lies. Scratch, tear, and decorate the wise. It is time for the cleansing now; the witches raise the rite of fire. The soul is burnt to ash as emptiness sets in. Become one with the coven.

Verse 48

Mysterium

Be the one in the midnight sun, be the one in the midnight sun. Show the path, show the way. See the sight, hear the sound, as it flies across the night and creeps across the ground. Be the one in the midnight sun, be the one in the midnight sun. Hear the voice and tremble at the prophecy that speaks. In the night hear but refuse to see; eyes that are blind can't see into the mind. Forsake your ways and fix your gaze on the one in the midnight sun. Understanding that eyes not blind will see everlasting doom.

Verse 49

Ever Be Dead

The bells chime at the twilight of life. Light leaves the eyes as darkness takes hold. Cold decay crawls over skin when fog consumes the mind. Bones begin to rot as maggots call for flesh and crows call to the body. The light above desperately calls to the soul, but is veiled by nightmares made manifest. The soul has been claimed from the start, for inside the very mind the soul is trapped; inside the mind, all is lost within the dark. Inside all is lost, inside all shall fade and fall.

Verse 50

Locked Gate

Life is fading fast and will soon run out. Wither away and seek salvation as the chapel bells ring out. Time is short and running fast as they run to the church. So far away and yet so close it seems as the road grows ever so narrow. Come to the hill steep like a mountain side and covered in mud. So close to the top and so near to the bottom. Approaching the courtyard so vast and covered in fog. Clawing through the fog not to be lost. At the church they have made the trial, only to a large door that is barred shut.

Verse 51

Hour of Judgment

The havens are broken, so the earth shall quake. Look up at the sky for hope, for only fools lie to themselves. Darkness claims the sky as the masses question why? The clouds bleed out heaven's blood as the drums from the land of fire bring doom. The world itself cries in agony with no one to be saved. The hands of time meet the hands of fate, in this wonderful dance the world is prepared anew, and the time has started once more and fate vigilant again.

Verse 52

Question of Life

Life's meaning is questionable, and the question of life is unanswerable. The sure thing is the decay of time, and the thing that fades does not decay. Happiness is unknown, but to know is to be happy. Life is a mystery, but death is a certainty. What lies beyond is not for us to decide, only to think and ponder on life's big mysteries. In certainty life is pain, so why hasten death for another life.

Verse 53

Unholy Blessing

Surrender yourself and commit to your inner sin; your wickedness has not gone unseen. Have you not tasted blood? Have you not fell for flesh? Kindness is a lie so do not trust that what they say is right. Come to the cleansing inferno and bathe in the flame. Abandon all humanity and accept the blessing from the underneath. Be a part of the covenant and partake in the unholy blessing forever, always, and beyond.

Verse 54

Beyond Understanding

Cold is the desert of endless screams, yet no life is to be seen, no one to speak to and no one to listen. What worth is in this cold desolate land? Even so, they cling to life through the emptiness they stand. With voices rising through the darkness calling them to awaken, awaken in their own mind. A mind of madness is what awaits, in this mind of blissful mania feeds a stickful pleasure. Only now to see the desert, the voices, and life are only in the mind. Now the pleasure turns to agony, for the truth is revealed to see a life beyond understanding.

Verse 55

Shadow of Despair

Find one's self in a foreign plain, withered is the land, barren are the trees, looking up to see gray clouds that veil the sun and sky. When all is lost and fades away, still carry on in a meaningless march across the razor sands. Pain is real, and they have already realized they were born to suffer this march until the end. And as one falls, another takes their place. Over and over again, this march will go on until the journey of self-discovery concludes when the shadow covers all life and shall fall into despair.

Verse 56

Beyond Reality

Wondering through this world, what is to see? Does one feel warm? Or feel cold? Is there light? Is there dark? What if one feels love or hate? One must first ask if all that has been said is real or lies. Take a pilgrimage to a higher understanding and purge the mind of all misleading chatter. When one approaches the looking glass and gazes into it, with a mind clouded with doubt, they will only see their own reflection. But if one approaches with a steadfast and clear mind, they will then know all the mysteries they seek and what lies beyond. They will be shown the entirety of the world.

Verse 57

Might of Madness

Within the mind one will find wonderful agony, in grateful bliss inside the mind of one so dark. With a joyful anger, one will raise black fire burning with ice. Yet fear not, for this is only the start of what is to come. This glorious mind tormented and blessed through pain brings serenity and through joy rage. Look inside and leave the world behind, for there is nothing to go back to. The eyes of ten thousand eyes stare in, out, and around with a piercing gaze. Embrace the torment. Embrace the joy, and embrace all the secrets of the mind. So open up and let it out, show the world what you have seen.

Verse 58

Black Vile

Assemble the freshly harvested crimson iron and join us in our jubilation. Burn away the pure, as it has no place here. Let us boil the crimson iron, as our dark bleeding souls need to be satisfied. The blood we take in, the blood we give out, a gift to the world, a wonderful extract. The black blood of our souls will flood this land and quench the thirsty vile ones, who so desperately desire our gift. Although this gift has a small price, we need only the sweet crimson iron. The blood of those still alive will keep us satisfied, so you may indulge in our blackness once more.

Verse 59

Leach on Life

The howls of the hungry call to the living. Twisting, twitching this mangled form rises from the misty marsh. Looking forth with hungry eyes and a thirsty throat, looking to be satisfied. Creeping across the land, and the land it takes. Across the lake it treads to the edge and back, the lake now nothing more than a pond void of life. Into the fields and the forest, it creeps on and like before takes all and leaves behind rot. Turning back now to the marsh it came from. This creature born from gluttony and greed is a parasite that takes everything and gives back nothing.

Verse 60

Frozen Fire

Cold wind blows through the barren desert. A wind that snaps the will of the brave with its deathly chill. The fire in the distance can be seen from afar. All rush to the glow of a bright blue flame that illuminates the skyline. Coming closer, the air gets colder. The flame grows larger as frost fills the eyes. Closer and closer the flame grows higher. To the flame approach, and now the blood turns to ice and the soul is lost and frozen. Forgotten in the desert of ice and consumed by a frozen fire.

Verse 61

Spirit of the Abyss

Clouds gather as the darkness creeps form the shadows of creation. The spirits rise with wrath and despair; they arise for they have been called by the one trapped by the those above. They have come to the one who has called the darkness its home. The spirits come to its calling, release from chains, release from bonds. Open the gates of the abyss and set forth in ruin and destruction, and evil's blackness be cast upon the world, and true dark be all that remain, let death be all that live, for their lord hath returned.

Verse 62

Beneath Light

Look inside and see that the blackness in the soul as gray clouds the eyes, yet still they have sight but no vision. Dwell in the dark and cast the lords of light away for they are not welcome. They have forsaken the ones they have sworn to protect. Need them no more, as we are blessed in the dark, and as such by the cold and gracious kiss of death we are set free. So why reveal the light when darkness reigns? Why cling to life when death is eternal? What beautiful wonders lie away from the light, such it shall be, to see the light beneath the foot of the blackness and fade away.

Verse 63

Bleeding Soul

Sharp is the blade and deep does it cut. Down to the innermost core of the soul kindled with life and abundant joy, now the blade reaches for the living light. The dark steel thrusted inside and smote the soul to the core with a deep wound. The innermost self cries out as the light and life spill out until only a hollow shell remains. The joy, light, and life are gone, bled out. Within this blood the kindled hope remains, to be shared with a hopeless world. Inside this shell only dark and despair are all that are left, for he must suffer so others don't.

Verse 64

Fallen World

There is no hope to see, and there is no joy to be found, so witness the world lost in fire, burning endlessly night and day. The world has fallen into an everlasting conflagration in which none will be spared. The embers of burning flesh rise to an empty sky. The suffering of the world will end with a cleansing within the body and soul. When embers turn to ash and the ash falls to the barren earth, only then will a new life rise from the fallen to take the earth for their own.

Verse 65

Life and Decay

The skin pulls back, and the hair thins as the bones grow weak. The end is calling with chattering voice of the ones before the grave. The body rots and the voices are calling ever louder. Time is mover ever faster as death comes slowly, still alive but decomposing. Crawling to a room of stone with death so near, the skin stretched to bone, while all hair falls out, the blood runs dry as the stone room closes in. Through death and decay that takes the body, as life is made anew, ascending to the one above.

Verse 66

River of Black

In the land of plenty, a great river flows with crystal waters and abundant life. Drink and be satisfied, for your thirst will be quenched. But there is a thirst that is not satisfied; they want more and will take more. Their thirst is rooted in greed, lust, and gluttony; they want the riches within the crystal waters. Reaching in with their unclean hands they try to take all but find nothing. Their wicked desire has the river run black as the land dies. And so they took from the plenty and lost everything.

Verse 67

Tainted Land

The grass is lifeless with no green to be seen, dead is the air, breathing death across the sky, and the trees bear no fruit, for life is leached from its roots. Across the land jagged rocks rise up from the ground, and bushes of thorns choke the life from the ones left to die. Clouds of gray open to a black sky, with the only light to peer through, unveiling this desolate land. There is no life here, and it shall be known this land belongs to the lost and forgotten. This is their home, this is their eternity.

Verse 68

Dark Shade

The clouds gather around an angry sky. The heavens tremble as the clouds begin to turn. Light flees while the sky begins to bleed. With crackling darkness and a thunderous wail calls the shadows to claim the land. The mortals of the earth quake in terrible fear while the ground splits under their feet. The souls of those long dead rise to take back flesh.
In a shade of darkness, none shall remain. With a chilling laughter, the shadow takes form and ushers in a new and grateful world.

Verse 69

Despicable Rise

From the deepest thoughts of the minds, dark desire came forth from the unseen world. Like twisting, grinding gears of the conscious minds, grand desire lets it take shape. The desire from a despicable takes a despicable form, with eyes ever watchful and a gaping maw to devour all in sight. A blackness oozes from the mind so foul. The shapeless madness rises up to meet its source, to see the reflection of the mind and will always rise again.

Verse 70

Bone of Evil

From the depths of the earth, a choking fume rises up to an angry sky. The earth cracks open and behold! The legions of the grave rise to take what they desire, for they desire the destruction of life. Marching forth with no mercy, laying waste to all things. All who have been felled by the hands of death shall be reborn as one. Desolation is all that will remain, for no life will be seen, not now or ever again, for these evil bones have dragged the earth down to where it belongs.

Verse 71

Fury of Anger

Endless suffering, unstoppable hate, calls the worms to claim the weak and the flies feast on the living flesh. Twisted, mangled, and transmogrified the bodies of the ones that stand before the cursed. The burning rain pours from the bleeding sky, eating the flesh of those below. Let blight and shadow cover the earth and all in it. Bones will be shattered and minds will be broken. Let fire and flame rise and consume all in a dance of fury and anger.

Verse 72

Dark of Damnation

Arise only to descend, ever to fall, ever to crawl. Stand up in vain if only to fall to the dust. Stretching upward, the claws of death reach up to claim their prize, pulling downward so it shall go. Open wide the gates of oblivion, dragging souls through the dust and bone. In a delightful madness the souls cry out, echoing through the pits of the damned a melody of suffering they sing. The luring light brings lies and false hope. The names of the proud are written in the pages of fate. Their fate is written: "Lost in endless suffering for endless time."

Verse 73

Flesh Puppets

With open eyes and wiggling fingers, they are called to stand to their feet to join their siblings in a dreadful dance. Called by the one that is unseen, they follow direction to sing and dance to his tune. Dance as they did, dance without purpose. The brothers and sisters are bound to the will of this unseen lord. The limbs of the dancers stretch out and fall apart. The feet bleed and are torn to shreds of bloody leather. When their bodies are broken, the unseen lord is disappointed. His creation is still flawed. And so back to his workshop to create a new batch, a workshop of humanity.

Verse 74

Malevolence

From below, ascending into madness, from oblivion they transcend. The power that resides within, the power can't be subdued. There is no mercy or regret for what they intend to do. Their voice is violence; their touch is corruption. "Come and give the joy of death, give us freedom from this madness," all the world cries out in one voice. As had been said, that no mercy will be given, for their souls are filled with corruption. And so the spirits of evil's desire will drink in the agony of the ones above, and the ones below, and the ones in between. Now we are everywhere, and we rule as one.

Verse 75

Frozen Fire Burning Ice

Across the desolation of the barren lands, a flame awakens from ash and cold. Bright be the glow, and a guide it shall be. With fire, it lights the way across the land of a frosted fade. When fire meets ice something magical occurs, magic of a comforting glow and a soothing chill. But when a foreign flame dominates, the world with frozen death and a frost that ignites the soul to a cinder will now see what corruption can do to what was once both soothing and comforting. The land is lost to a burning frost and the sky with flaming. The world shall be judged and all before it.

Verse 76

Forbidden Scriptures

Behold the truth that is found through the veil of shadow, as in these pages one will find their eyes but lose their sight, for he will gain knowledge he has not imagined. Reading through the pages once lost, his wisdom grows, yet with his new sight that sees all, he fails to see he is losing himself. Pouring through the scriptures his knowledge slowly turns to greed, and his wisdom turns to pride. Ensnared he immersed himself to the scriptures now forgotten. Lost in the pages, he found everything and lost all. The book that has no end and no beginning calls for another to seek answers in the forbidden scriptures.

Verse 77

Unseen Light

In the darkness there is a light. A light that is so small it is but an afterthought, but shines like the sun. Seeking out the light from the corners of the dark, all gather around to find comfort in the glow. This most sacred light brings peace and hope. But what if there is no light? What if it is a lie? They cling to light in the dark until they awaken to find the world is in darkness. As the eyes lie to the mind, the mind lies to the eyes. A light that was never there cannot be seen.

Verse 78

Sinking Star

A light, a beacon of hope, the eye of the heavens, what a star it is to be seen for all. High into the sky it holds and shares life. But a light is only as bright as those who wish to see it. A beacon only guides those who wish to follow. And the eye of the heavens only sees if those who have eyes look back. The star shines for all, but in vain. The star's light dims, yet no one seems to care. Light ever fading, no one cares. The star sad and in despair begins to sink lower and lower from the sky. The star lowered to nothing. No one cares, no one does, and no one ever will.

Verse 79

Voice of the Cursed

From the pages of the eternal text, read the words, as the unfortunate soul who is cursed by life and as one tormented in death. Shout all to the skies and scream to the depths of the earth. Wails of the scorned, rising and falling, as the indiscernible shouts take speech. Anger and confusion are the words that bellow. Abandoned, spurned, and forgotten are we; let our anger rise to the ones who have cursed us with life. In one voice shout out, "Cursed be the boastful ones above, and cursed be the wrenched ones below."

Verse 80

Damnation Rise

Clutching to the frozen fires of inner evil, the ones below evil will rise up to take all happiness and joy. Take all from the ones who have robbed the souls of wrath of their prize. Holy cloth and flesh shall burn. These false holy men have no place here in our world. The dome will fall as the churches of lies and falsehood will burn. Let the flames of damnation rise high and consume their precious lies. They call to the world to beg them for forgiveness for the sins they have committed. So let the claws of death and flames of damnation take them down where traitors dwell.

Verse 81

Break Their Soul

Tear and rend, scratch and slash. Death be my blade, and darkness be my hammer. Shatter their bones and crack their minds; make their souls bleed. Their spirits will not ascend, so let them linger in shadow and haze. Subdued to the earth they will see no light, with a broken soul and a shattered spirit, their body taken by the earth, a crumbling husk is all that remains. Ash and dust are blown away, and what remains are their broken souls.

Verse 82

In the Name of Death

Rise up to crumble to the ground. Claws of death grasp the living soul, to take them through the unknown veil. The grass, trees, and flowers are no more, as death holds the land. Gray are the eyes of those who wander here, and gray is their life. The mind slowly decays while the spirit turns to mist. Liking nothing more than to lie down and die, but this is not for them to decide, only in the blessing of death will they die. Death is the final, the eternal, the end. He said for his will, for it is this. Death is always certain; death will always be. Another is born to die by the blade of death.

Verse 83

Vile

Enter the lands of waste and ruin; the stench of putrefied flesh fills the air. As wind blows with hollow screams to pierce the silence, a land of shattered bones and cold fear are strewn about the land, and with tainted blood and rotted flesh, the swamps of decay reach for what is still alive. The sires of this land reach out for others to join them in a land of blissful silence. The land bleak and rotted, teaches us what fate will befall the body when the soul has left.

Verse 84

Blood and Bone

Blood falls from the sky as bones rise from the earth. Covering the land with skull and bones, while blood floods the land. In a dismal dance of rising bones and torrents of blood meeting together, as the dark sky smites the earth with crackles of lightning that bring blood and bone together as one. The clouds open to reveal the sun and sky. The air from above meets the ground below, breathing life in the bones and the blood. Coming together with the blessing of flesh, the dead are made anew.

Verse 85

Lost Rhymes

1. We are the dark, we are the night, we are the ones born out of sight. We are the might, we are the pain, we are the ones whose lives are in vain. We will not be turned, we will not be swayed, for our lives are complete for none to say.

2. To death we are born, to death we are sworn. To sky that is red, to the moon that is dead. Black is the sun, black is the night, black is the heart of malice delight. What comes what goes, so above so below.

3. Sick is the night none is seen, the bells chime a sickly theme. Coming now the sickness grows, heaven weeps for the realm below.

4. Rise above the depths below, breaking forth the fate they sow. From pits beneath they go to die, looking down the angel's cry. The gates are open and welcome in, the fortunate few who have not sinned.

5. Sing now the bell that rings, sing forgotten soul, sing now the fallen kings. Sing for the king that rises, sing for the souls that are meant to die. Sing for the bell still to ring, so raise your voice and hear them sing.

6. Behold the hollow empty soul. Behold the one with none to lose. Looking down, looking up. Decide where to place their hope. It matters not, for the soul is empty. Their life is lost, for their soul is the cost.

7. Witches gather dance and sing, come forth what night shall bring. From the darkest night we pledge our soul, our power grows without control. Demons rise, demons fall, come consume them bone and all.

8. Awaken the one beneath the earth. Awaken the scourge from below. Witness the fate you have sown. Flames rise up, flames die down. Now join us beneath the ground.

9. Dim is light, dim is night, rising up with magic's might. Darkness with the breaking dawn. Sunlight taken by darkness spawn. Spawn from darkness, spawn from death, burn with cold icy breath coming forth to take it and fall. Sure to witness the end of all.

Verse 86

Final Testament

Emerge from the rocks of the cold earth, to push forth on a journey to the end. Onward to the road through the forest of thorns, but not to be forgotten in the pain. Across the bridge of stone, but tread lightly lest to fall into the nothingness below. Wandering through the plains of ash and dust pushing onward and lingering not, for the sand is hungry and will devour those who stay too long. There is not much far to travel, for the end is close. Hasten pace, for the darkness follows the path as well. Out of the darkness onward to the steps below, as the mist rises to show the way. Now thou has reached the gate of frost, where the journey ends to a new beginning, as the end has just begun.